Study Guide

Social Psychology